MAYER SMITH

The Nightborn Prince and the Dawn Touched Maiden

Copyright © 2025 by Mayer Smith

All rights reserved. No part of this publication may be reproduced, stored or transmitted in any form or by any means, electronic, mechanical, photocopying, recording, scanning, or otherwise without written permission from the publisher. It is illegal to copy this book, post it to a website, or distribute it by any other means without permission.

This novel is entirely a work of fiction. The names, characters and incidents portrayed in it are the work of the author's imagination. Any resemblance to actual persons, living or dead, events or localities is entirely coincidental.

Mayer Smith asserts the moral right to be identified as the author of this work.

Mayer Smith has no responsibility for the persistence or accuracy of URLs for external or third-party Internet Websites referred to in this publication and does not guarantee that any content on such Websites is, or will remain, accurate or appropriate.

Designations used by companies to distinguish their products are often claimed as trademarks. All brand names and product names used in this book and on its cover are trade names, service marks, trademarks and registered trademarks of their respective owners. The publishers and the book are not associated with any product or vendor mentioned in this book. None of the companies referenced within the book have endorsed the book.

First edition

*This book was professionally typeset on Reedsy.
Find out more at reedsy.com*

Contents

1	The Gathering of Shadows	1
2	Whispers in the Wind	7
3	The Mark of the Sun	13
4	A Pact with Darkness	19
5	Secrets in the Forest of Echoes	26
6	The Silent Guardian	32
7	The Breaking Dawn	39
8	The Betrayal of the Silver King	46
9	The Shadowed Heart	53
10	The Dance of Light and Dark	60
11	The Heart of Betrayal	66
12	The Shattered Oath	73
13	The Betrayer's Blade	79
14	The Fall of Night	86
15	The Last Light	92

One

The Gathering of Shadows

The night air was thick with the scent of jasmine and moonlit earth as Lyra moved silently through the tangled undergrowth of the forbidden garden. The whispered rustle of leaves seemed to echo in the stillness, like the murmurs of a thousand voices, each carrying a secret too dangerous to utter aloud. Her heart pounded in her chest, not from fear but from the electrifying thrill of being here, of walking where none from her village dared to tread.

Above her, the blood-red moon hung low in the sky, casting an eerie glow over the grounds of the estate, a place only spoken of in rumors and hushed voices. Tonight, the barrier between the world of the living and the unknown was thinnest, and the air seemed alive with possibility. Tonight, everything would change.

Lyra's fingers brushed against the smooth stone of a hidden archway, and she paused. From here, she could hear faint laughter and music drifting from beyond the garden's high walls. The invitations to this gathering were as rare as they were dangerous. No one had been invited by accident, and no one would leave unchanged.

With a deep breath, she pushed forward. The world around her seemed to bend, the shadows stretching longer as if to swallow her whole. But she didn't turn back. Not now. Not when she had already made it this far.

The gathering was held in the heart of the estate, within the grand ballroom where only the most powerful and enigmatic of the Nightborn gathered. It was a place for the elite, a sanctuary for those whose power came from the darkest corners of the earth. She had never seen it with her own eyes, but tonight, she would.

The doors of the ballroom loomed before her—tall, wrought iron and crowned with silver designs that shimmered as if alive. She could hear voices now, a low hum of conversation mixed with the occasional clink of glass. They were waiting for something, or someone, though she wasn't certain. She only knew that once she stepped through those doors, there would be no turning back.

Lyra's breath caught as she placed her hand on the cold metal handle, feeling the weight of the decision pressing down on her. She had come here seeking answers, but part of her feared what she might discover. What if she wasn't ready for the truth?

The Gathering of Shadows

What if it shattered the world she had known, the world she had fought so hard to protect?

But there was no more time to hesitate. She gripped the handle and pushed the doors open.

The room beyond was nothing like she had imagined.

Lush red velvet draped over every surface, and tall, flickering candles lined the walls, casting the room in a warm, amber light that seemed to dance with a life of its own. The guests were elegant, their masks hiding their true faces, their attire a mix of shimmering silks and dark, shadowy fabrics that seemed to absorb the light rather than reflect it.

And then, there he was.

At the far end of the room, Kaelen stood like a shadow among the flames. His presence alone seemed to draw the darkness around him, the air growing colder as if the room itself was holding its breath. He wore a mask of obsidian, his sharp features obscured but still unmistakable. His eyes—those eyes—shone like twin stars, bright and unreadable, glimmering with an intensity that made her stomach flutter.

Lyra knew who he was. Everyone did. The Nightborn Prince. The heir to the ancient bloodline of shadow and darkness.

She had heard the rumors. She had heard of the terrible power that lay within him, the curse that had tainted his soul, and the destruction he was destined to bring.

But none of that stopped her from walking toward him.

Her steps were slow, deliberate, each one echoing in the silence that had fallen over the room as she made her way forward. She was acutely aware of the gazes that followed her, the eyes of the other guests hidden behind masks, their thoughts unreadable, but the weight of their scrutiny was impossible to ignore.

Kaelen didn't move as she approached. His expression was unreadable, his stance as still as a statue, but his eyes... they were locked on hers. The connection between them was instantaneous, and Lyra felt a shiver run through her, as if something deep within her had recognized him for who he truly was.

Her pulse quickened.

"You've come," his voice was a low murmur, rough and smooth all at once, like the sound of a storm breaking over a distant sea.

Lyra's breath caught in her throat. She hadn't spoken a word, yet he knew she was here. He had been waiting for her.

"I wasn't sure I would," she replied, her voice trembling despite her best efforts to remain calm. She had prepared for this moment, rehearsed the words she might say, but now that she stood before him, they seemed inadequate. How could she speak when every fiber of her being was telling her that this moment was far larger than anything she could have anticipated?

Kaelen took a step closer, his gaze unwavering. The crowd parted as he moved, the air around him shifting, as if the room itself were adjusting to his presence.

"You've made a dangerous choice," he said, his voice laced with something like warning. "Do you understand that?"

Lyra's breath faltered, and she couldn't help but glance over her shoulder at the door she had just entered. Was it too late to leave? Was it too late to escape whatever was beginning to stir between them?

"I don't know what I'm walking into," she admitted, her voice barely above a whisper.

His lips curled into a smile—half-pity, half-amusement—and for a brief moment, it seemed as though he might say something else, something that could shatter her resolve entirely.

But then, the moment was interrupted.

A loud crash sounded from across the room, followed by a burst of laughter that was more cruel than jovial. The guests around them began to murmur, some stepping away, others moving closer as if the disruption was part of the game they were all playing.

Kaelen didn't flinch. He simply turned, his eyes narrowing as he looked toward the source of the disturbance.

Lyra felt a cold chill settle over her as the room seemed to darken just a fraction more. The chaos was beginning—unseen forces moving in the shadows, unknown dangers stirring beneath the surface.

She had been warned, but now, standing in the heart of this world, she felt the weight of the prophecy settle around her like a noose.

Her gaze flickered back to Kaelen, and she saw the uncertainty flicker in his eyes too, though he quickly masked it with the practiced coolness of a prince born into darkness. He was a master of control, and she was just a pawn.

The game had only just begun. And in this place, there was no telling who would be left standing when the final move was made.

Two

Whispers in the Wind

The soft breeze tugged at Lyra's hair as she stood in the quiet meadow just outside the estate. The morning light had barely begun to touch the edges of the sky, but already, a sense of unease clung to the air like a heavy mist. It was as though the world was holding its breath, waiting for something to happen—something Lyra couldn't quite grasp.

She pulled her cloak tighter around her shoulders, the fabric stiff against her skin. The memory of last night's gathering still lingered in her mind, an intoxicating mixture of fear and fascination. Kaelen's presence had haunted her throughout the night, his words echoing in the silence of her dreams. But it wasn't just his voice. It was the feeling—the sensation of something dark and ancient stirring within her, something she hadn't yet understood.

Shivering despite the warmth of the sun on her skin, Lyra took a few tentative steps forward, her boots sinking softly into the dew-covered grass. The whispers came again. Low at first, almost imperceptible, like the rustling of leaves in a windless night. But as she moved further from the estate, the whispers grew louder, curling around her like tendrils of smoke.

"Lyra…"

She froze. The voice was faint, almost lost in the breeze, but it was unmistakable. Her name—spoken with an urgency that chilled her to the bone. She spun around, heart pounding, but the meadow was empty. There was no one there.

"Lyra…" The voice came again, clearer this time, as if it were just behind her, a breath away from her ear. She whipped her head to the side, her pulse thrumming in her throat.

Nothing.

She stood still, trying to steady her breathing. Was it the wind playing tricks on her, or was it something else? Something… supernatural?

Her eyes scanned the horizon, the rolling hills stretching into the distance, but there was no sign of movement. Nothing except the rustling of the trees, the shifting of shadows as the day began to break. Still, the whispers persisted, faint but unmistakable, as if they were coming from deep within the earth itself.

Whispers in the Wind

"Who's there?" she called out, her voice trembling slightly, betraying the fear that had begun to crawl up her spine.

No answer.

The wind carried a strange chill with it now, cutting through her cloak as though it had a mind of its own. Lyra took another step forward, determined to shake the feeling of being watched, but it only intensified. The whispers were growing louder, surrounding her on all sides.

"Lyra…"

She couldn't breathe. The air felt too thick, like it was pressing down on her chest, each breath a struggle. Her mind raced—was this the beginning of the prophecy? Had she already been marked by whatever fate lay in store for her?

She tried to calm herself, to push away the fear that had suddenly gripped her heart, but her feet felt as though they were rooted to the ground, the whispers pulling her deeper into the meadow. It was then that she heard a sound that cut through the whispers like a knife—a single, sharp rustle of leaves.

She turned swiftly, her eyes darting toward the source of the noise. And there, standing at the edge of the clearing, was Kaelen.

His presence seemed to distort the very air around him, casting a long shadow that stretched impossibly far. His eyes—those strange, haunting eyes—locked onto hers, and for a moment,

Lyra forgot to breathe. It was as though the rest of the world had ceased to exist, leaving only the two of them, standing in the silence of the meadow.

"Kaelen..." she whispered, her voice shaky, though she wasn't sure why. It wasn't fear she felt when she looked at him—it was something darker, something that pulled her in, deeper with each passing second.

He took a slow step toward her, his gaze never leaving hers. "You hear them too, don't you?" His voice was low, edged with something that made Lyra's pulse quicken, a sense of danger coiling beneath his words.

"Whispers?" she asked, barely managing to keep her voice steady. "Is that... is that you?"

"No," Kaelen said, the single word laced with a bitter laugh. "It's not me. It's them."

Lyra took a tentative step backward, the ground beneath her feet shifting ever so slightly. Something was wrong. The air felt heavier, charged with a strange energy, and Kaelen's presence only seemed to make it worse. Her skin prickled as if a thousand invisible eyes were watching them, hidden just beyond the reach of sight.

"Who are they?" she asked, her voice barely audible against the oppressive stillness of the meadow.

Kaelen's gaze flickered briefly to the sky before returning to her, his expression unreadable. "The spirits. The ones that linger in the wind. They are restless. They are calling to you."

Lyra frowned, her mind racing. Spirits? Was this what the sorcerer had warned her about? The ancient forces that tied her fate to the dark realm Kaelen came from?

"But why me?" she asked, her voice sharp now, betraying the growing panic in her chest.

Kaelen didn't answer immediately. Instead, he took another step closer, and Lyra found herself rooted to the spot, unable to move even if she wanted to. He stood just inches from her now, and despite the warmth of the sun creeping over the horizon, a cold shiver ran down her spine.

"Because they are afraid," he said softly. "Afraid of what you might become."

Before she could ask him what he meant, a sudden gust of wind blew through the meadow, and the whispers reached a crescendo, as if a thousand voices were speaking in unison.

Lyra's eyes widened as the wind seemed to twist around her, pulling at her cloak, tugging at her hair. The earth beneath her feet trembled, just for a heartbeat, and then... it was gone.

The silence that followed was deafening. The meadow was still once again, the sun now fully risen, casting its light on everything as if nothing had happened.

Kaelen stood before her, his expression unreadable. The whispers had stopped, but Lyra couldn't shake the feeling that something had changed. Something had shifted in the air, something dark and ancient, something that had been set in motion the moment she had crossed the threshold into his world.

"What was that?" Lyra whispered, the question escaping her lips before she could stop herself.

Kaelen's eyes flickered, and for a moment, she saw something there—something almost like pity, before it was quickly masked by his usual, cold composure.

"You should have stayed away," he said quietly. "Now they know your name."

Three

The Mark of the Sun

Lyra woke in a cold sweat, her heart pounding in her chest. The room around her was shrouded in darkness, save for the faint glow of the moon casting slivers of silver through her window. The nightmares had returned, their grip tighter than ever before. Shadows had danced across her mind, and Kaelen's face—his haunting, unreadable gaze—had appeared again, lingering like a shadow at the edges of her dream.

But it wasn't just his presence that unsettled her. It was the mark.

She could still feel the heat of it, burning into her skin, though she had not yet seen it with her own eyes. The whispers from the meadow, the ones that had called her name, had spoken of it. She had never believed in prophecies or ancient curses, but there was no denying what was happening to her now. Something had changed. Something had awakened, and she was no longer sure if she could control it.

Sitting up in bed, she pushed her tangled hair out of her face and swung her legs over the side. The cold floor beneath her feet sent a shiver up her spine, but she didn't care. The whispers still echoed in her ears, their words unclear but undeniably urgent.

She had to see it.

With trembling hands, she grabbed the edge of her nightgown and pulled it over her head, exposing her bare skin. In the dim light, she could just make out the faint outline of a mark on her left wrist—something that hadn't been there before. A symbol, delicate yet somehow insistent, shaped like the sun, but with rays that curved inwards, like the tendrils of a vine.

Her breath caught in her throat.

It was the mark she had seen in the old texts—those cryptic warnings about the Dawn Touched. Her pulse quickened as she traced the symbol with a finger, the lines burning slightly under her touch, as if the mark itself were alive.

"Lyra…"

The voice was faint at first, like a memory rising from the depths of her subconscious. But this time, it wasn't just in her mind. She could hear it, feel it in the air around her, a vibration that made the hairs on her arms stand on end.

The Mark of the Sun

The mark. It was connected to the whispers. And now, it was calling her.

But to where? And for what?

The questions swirled in her mind, and she knew she couldn't ignore them any longer. She had to find answers—answers that could be buried deeper than she was willing to admit. The mark, the whispers, the feeling that something dark and ancient had been set in motion when she crossed paths with Kaelen—it was all tangled together, pulling her into a world she had no understanding of.

With a deep breath, she slipped her robe on and hurried out of the room, her footsteps muffled by the thick carpets. She moved through the halls of the estate, her heart thumping louder with every step she took. The servants were already awake, their soft murmurs echoing through the corridors, but no one seemed to notice her.

She reached the library—a vast room filled with towering shelves of books—and paused just outside the heavy oak door. There was no one inside, save for the ancient tomes that lined the walls. She had spent hours in here before, reading about the ancient powers and the realms beyond her own, but she had never thought the stories could be real.

She stepped inside, her eyes scanning the familiar rows of books. She knew what she was looking for, even if she didn't fully understand it. She had to find more about the Dawn Touched—about the mark and its meaning.

Her fingers ran over the spines of the books, some old and dusty, others more recent, their pages yellowed with age. She pulled down one at random, flipping through the pages until a passage caught her eye. It was a story, one she had read before but had dismissed as myth.

The Dawn Touched were marked from birth, their fate intertwined with the balance of the realms. A symbol of the sun, their mark would reveal itself when the time was right, when the world was at its most vulnerable. They were the protectors, but also the harbingers of doom.

Lyra's breath hitched. She could feel the words sinking deep into her chest, settling like stones in her stomach. This was no simple curse—it was her fate. And with it came something far darker than she had realized.

She closed the book with a snap and turned to leave, her mind reeling. But as she moved toward the door, she stopped short. A figure stood in the doorway, blocking her exit.

It was Kaelen.

His presence filled the room like a shadow, the air growing colder with each passing second. His eyes—those intense, otherworldly eyes—locked onto hers, and for a moment, the world seemed to disappear. The space between them seemed to crackle with an energy neither of them could control.

"What are you doing here?" Lyra asked, her voice sharp, though it wavered under the weight of his gaze.

Kaelen didn't answer right away. Instead, he stepped further into the room, his movements fluid, almost predatory. His cloak swirled around him like smoke, the edges shifting with an unnatural grace. There was something about him tonight—something different.

"I've been watching you," he said, his voice low and steady, but there was an edge to it, something dangerous lurking beneath.

Lyra's breath caught in her throat. "What do you want from me?"

Kaelen's gaze flickered to the book in her hand, then back to her face. "You know why I'm here. You've seen the mark. You felt it, didn't you?"

Lyra's heart skipped a beat. She had not told him about the mark, had not even dared to speak of it to anyone, but somehow, Kaelen knew.

The whispers came again, louder this time, swirling around them like a storm, filling the room with their clamoring voices. Lyra took a step back, her pulse racing.

"Why is it calling me?" she asked, her voice barely above a whisper.

Kaelen's expression darkened, and for a moment, Lyra saw something in his eyes—something that wasn't just cold and distant, but regret. "It's not the mark that's calling you. It's the curse."

Lyra's breath faltered. "What curse?"

"The curse that binds us," he said, his voice tight with something she couldn't quite place. "The curse that has been waiting for you."

Suddenly, the ground beneath her feet trembled, just slightly, as though the earth itself was reacting to his words. Lyra steadied herself, her hands gripping the book tighter.

"What do you mean?" she asked, her voice thick with fear. "What curse?"

Kaelen's lips parted as if he might answer, but before he could, the room darkened, the candles flickering violently as an unnatural wind swept through the library, slamming the doors shut with a deafening crash.

A voice—low, guttural, and filled with malice—ripped through the air.

"The time has come."

Lyra spun around, her heart thundering in her chest. The shadows in the corners of the room seemed to writhe, stretching, bending, as though something was emerging from them. Kaelen stepped forward, his eyes flashing with a strange intensity.

"They're here," he said, barely above a whisper. "And now, so are you."

Four

A Pact with Darkness

The moon was full, casting its pale glow across the dense forest surrounding the estate. The trees stood like sentinels, their twisted limbs clawing at the sky, their shadows stretching long across the forest floor. The air was thick with the scent of damp earth and the musky odor of old leaves. A heavy stillness had settled over the woods, as though the night itself was holding its breath, waiting for something to unfold.

Lyra's steps were silent as she moved through the underbrush, her feet brushing over the soft, wet ground. She had not planned to come here, not tonight, but the whispers had become impossible to ignore. The call had grown louder over the past few days, their words more insistent, demanding her attention. And now, in the dead of night, they had led her here, to this place—the ancient clearing in the heart of the forest.

The Nightborn Prince and the Dawn Touched Maiden

As she approached the clearing, her pulse quickened. The moonlight had pierced the canopy, casting a ghostly glow on the circle of stones that surrounded the area. The air seemed charged with energy, thick with an invisible force that made the hairs on the back of her neck stand on end. This was no ordinary forest. This was a place where the boundaries between the realms of light and dark were thin, where magic could be touched, twisted, and unleashed.

And yet, she couldn't turn back now. The mark on her wrist—the one that had burned beneath her skin ever since that night—was the reason she had come. It was the reason she had crossed paths with Kaelen, with the cursed prince who seemed to haunt her thoughts. She had tried to ignore it, tried to push the knowledge of what was happening to her deep down into the corners of her mind, but it was no use. She had been marked, and with that mark came a destiny she couldn't escape.

Her breath was shallow as she stepped into the center of the stone circle, the whispers swirling around her like a storm. They were louder now, more distinct, their words clearer than ever before. "Come… come to us…" the voices urged, soft and seductive.

The air grew colder, the chill creeping into her bones, and then, just as suddenly as it had begun, the whispers stopped. A silence so profound settled over the clearing that it felt as if the world had frozen.

A figure appeared from the shadows.

A Pact with Darkness

Lyra's breath caught in her throat as Kaelen stepped into the moonlight, his dark silhouette cutting through the shadows like a knife. His eyes—those piercing, silver eyes—glowed faintly, his expression unreadable. The wind shifted, tugging at his cloak, and for a brief moment, it seemed as though he was more shadow than flesh, more a specter than a man.

"You came," his voice was low, almost a growl, as though it was a surprise he hadn't expected.

Lyra swallowed hard, forcing herself to meet his gaze. "I had no choice," she said, her voice steady despite the fear twisting in her stomach. "The whispers—they led me here."

Kaelen studied her for a long moment, his gaze flickering to the mark on her wrist, which had begun to throb painfully. She couldn't help but flinch at the sudden, sharp pulse of heat that radiated from the symbol. It felt like something was waking inside her—something she didn't fully understand, but knew was tied to him. To the curse.

"You were meant to come," Kaelen said, his tone flat, but there was something else beneath it, something darker. "You always have been."

Lyra's heart skipped a beat. "What do you mean? What is this? What is happening to me?"

Kaelen took a step forward, his movements deliberate, like a predator circling its prey. "You are the key. The mark on your wrist, the bond between us—everything that has led you here has brought you to this moment." His voice dropped, the words becoming almost a whisper. "And now you have to choose."

Her breath hitched. "Choose what?"

Kaelen's eyes darkened. "A pact," he said, his words laced with a weight that seemed to press down on her chest. "A pact with the darkness. With me."

Lyra took a step back, her pulse racing. "What are you talking about?" she demanded, her voice trembling. She had heard rumors, of course—whispers in the village about ancient pacts, dark bargains struck by those desperate enough to seek power. But she had never truly believed in them. Not until now.

Kaelen's lips curled into a smile, but it was cold, devoid of warmth. "You don't have a choice, Lyra. The power that courses through you—the power of the Dawn Touched—has always been connected to the night. It's a balance, a dark and light that must coexist. But without the pact, the darkness will consume you."

Lyra recoiled. "What do you mean, it will consume me? I don't want any part of this. I never asked for it!"

Kaelen's gaze softened, but only slightly, and for a brief moment, she thought she saw something resembling regret in his eyes. "You never asked for it, no. But it's already inside you. It's in the mark, in your blood, in your fate. To control it, to wield it without succumbing to it… you need the pact."

A Pact with Darkness

The wind picked up again, swirling around them in a frenzy. Lyra closed her eyes, her mind racing. She had always believed she was ordinary—just a simple girl from the village with no ties to anything greater. But this... this curse, this bond to Kaelen, it shattered everything she had ever known.

"What do I have to do?" she asked, her voice barely a whisper, though the words felt like they were tearing at her from the inside.

Kaelen didn't answer right away. Instead, he stepped closer, the shadows seeming to shift with his movements, as if they were responding to him, bending and stretching to his will. "The pact is not easy," he said, his voice low and filled with an unspoken warning. "It requires a sacrifice."

Lyra's chest tightened. "A sacrifice? What kind of sacrifice?"

Kaelen didn't look away. "Your soul," he said simply. "Your soul, bound to mine, bound to the night."

Lyra's knees threatened to buckle beneath her, and she struggled to keep herself upright. "No," she whispered, shaking her head. "I won't do that. I won't give up my soul."

Kaelen's eyes flashed with something—anger, frustration, maybe even pity. But it was gone in an instant, replaced by the cold mask of the prince who had made the darkness his ally.

"You have no choice," he said, his voice hardening. "If you don't accept the pact, the darkness will consume you—and there will be nothing left of you to save."

The wind howled, the trees groaning under the pressure of the unseen force that surrounded them. Lyra could feel the weight of the decision pressing down on her, suffocating her. She wanted to run. To escape. But she knew that wasn't an option anymore. Not with the mark burning beneath her skin. Not with Kaelen standing before her, his dark magic weaving around them like an invisible thread, pulling her closer, making her feel as if there was no escape from the fate that had already been sealed.

She closed her eyes, her breath coming in ragged gasps. Was there any other choice? Could she fight it? Could she escape this fate?

When she opened her eyes again, Kaelen was standing even closer, his presence suffocating, his dark gaze unwavering.

"Make your choice, Lyra," he said softly. "The pact, or the darkness."

And in that moment, she realized the truth. The choice wasn't hers at all. She had already made it the moment she had stepped into the clearing. She was already bound to him. Bound to the darkness.

With trembling hands, she reached out, and as her fingers brushed his, she whispered the words she had hoped she would never have to speak.

A Pact with Darkness

"I accept."

And with that acceptance, the forest trembled, the ground beneath them shifting, as the pact was sealed.

Five

Secrets in the Forest of Echoes

The forest had changed.

Lyra stood at the edge of the clearing, her heart pounding in her chest as the world around her twisted and bent in ways that should not have been possible. The wind howled through the trees, but there was no relief from the chill that gripped her. The pact she had made with Kaelen—those words she had whispered in the dead of night—seemed to echo in the very air, reverberating like the final note of a song that had no end.

She could feel it now, the darkness that pulsed beneath her skin, like an ancient force coiling around her heart. The mark on her wrist had deepened, its rays now shifting in color, glowing faintly in the dim light of the moon. The power Kaelen had promised her was real, but it was also dangerous—far more dangerous than she had anticipated. And now, standing here, alone in the heart of the Forest of Echoes, she wondered if she had made a grave mistake.

A branch cracked behind her, snapping her from her thoughts. Lyra spun around, her pulse racing. Kaelen was there, standing at the edge of the clearing, his figure half-obscured by the darkness. His silver eyes gleamed, faintly glowing in the moonlight, but his expression was unreadable.

"Did you think you could escape?" His voice was a low, dangerous growl, carried on the wind like a whisper from the abyss. "You are bound to this place now. To me."

Lyra's breath caught in her throat. The air around them seemed to thicken, the very fabric of the forest holding its breath. Something ancient was stirring beneath the earth, deep in the roots of the trees, and Lyra could feel it. The forest was alive, watching, listening. The whispers she had heard since the pact had grown louder, more insistent, filling her mind with fractured images and fragmented memories.

"The mark…" she whispered, the words slipping from her lips before she could stop herself. "What does it mean? Why does it burn?"

Kaelen stepped forward, his eyes never leaving hers. He seemed to glide through the shadows, his every movement deliberate and unnervingly graceful. "It is the binding," he said, his voice almost gentle, as if trying to soothe a beast he had created. "You are mine now, Lyra. Your soul is intertwined with mine. The darkness will never leave you, but neither will the light. You are the bridge between the two worlds."

Her stomach churned. She had known what she was signing up for when she made the pact, but now that the weight of it was settling on her shoulders, the reality was more suffocating than she had imagined. The thought of being bound to him, to this prince of shadows, made her skin crawl, yet she could not deny the pull between them—the bond that seemed to tether her to him no matter how much she tried to resist.

"What do you want from me?" she demanded, her voice rising in desperation. "What am I supposed to do now?"

Kaelen didn't answer immediately. Instead, he stepped closer, his presence a heavy weight in the air. Lyra took a step back, instinctively, but the ground beneath her feet shifted, causing her to stumble. She reached out to steady herself, her fingers brushing against the bark of a nearby tree. It was cold—unnaturally cold. The tree seemed to shudder beneath her touch, its bark cracking like dry leaves.

Kaelen's eyes narrowed, and his lips curled into a faint, knowing smile. "You will learn to control the power inside you, Lyra. You will learn to embrace it. The Forest of Echoes will teach you."

Lyra's breath caught in her throat. "What is that supposed to mean?"

"You have entered the heart of the forest," Kaelen said, his voice now almost a whisper, as though speaking too loudly would disturb something ancient and powerful that lay hidden within the woods. "The spirits of this place are not like the others you've encountered. They have been here long before you or I. They are the guardians of the balance. And they will test you."

The words hung in the air like a weight. The wind seemed to die down for a moment, leaving an eerie silence in its wake. Lyra felt a sudden, overwhelming sense of dread as she realized that she wasn't alone. It wasn't just Kaelen in the clearing anymore. The forest itself was watching her, waiting.

A low hum began to fill the air, faint at first, like the sound of a distant drumbeat. But as it grew louder, Lyra realized it wasn't coming from outside the clearing. It was coming from the trees themselves. From the earth beneath her feet. The vibrations seemed to pulse in time with her heartbeat, and she felt a strange pressure on her chest, as though something was trying to break free.

The whispers returned, louder now, disembodied voices weaving through the wind, their words incomprehensible, but filled with a sense of urgency. Then, from the shadows of the trees, shapes began to form—faint, ethereal figures, their outlines blurred as if they were made of smoke. They moved silently, their eyes glowing with an unnatural light, watching her every move.

Lyra's breath caught in her throat as the figures circled her. Their gazes were piercing, unblinking, as if they could see straight into her soul. And in that moment, she understood.

They were the spirits of the forest, and they had come to judge her.

"Do not be afraid," Kaelen said, his voice low and steady, though the words felt like an echo in the vast emptiness of the clearing. "They will not harm you, not unless you fail."

"Fail?" Lyra repeated, her voice shaking. "Fail at what?"

"The trial," Kaelen said. "To prove you are worthy of the power inside you. To prove you are strong enough to carry the burden of the pact."

The spirits moved closer, their forms becoming more defined as they stepped into the moonlight. They were tall, almost humanoid in shape, but their features were blurred, indistinct, like shadows that couldn't quite hold their form. The air around them seemed to warp and shimmer, as though the very fabric of reality was bending under their presence.

One of the spirits raised a hand, and a low, resonant hum echoed through the clearing. Lyra felt the vibrations reverberate through her body, and suddenly, the forest seemed to come alive around her. The trees creaked and groaned, their branches reaching out like skeletal fingers. The ground trembled, as if something deep below the surface was awakening.

A wave of energy surged through her, and Lyra gasped, her knees buckling as the mark on her wrist flared to life, burning with an intensity she hadn't felt before. The pain was overwhelming, a searing fire that coursed through her veins, but beneath it, she could feel the darkness—coiling and twisting like a serpent, whispering promises of power, of freedom.

But she also felt something else. Something soft, something pure. The light that had always been a part of her, the light that the darkness sought to consume.

The spirits stepped closer, their eyes fixed on her, and in that moment, she knew they were waiting for her to make a choice. A choice that would determine her fate.

Lyra clenched her fists, her breath coming in ragged gasps. The darkness whispered louder, urging her to give in. To embrace the power, to allow the forest and the pact to consume her.

But the light inside her fought back, and for the first time since she had made the pact, Lyra felt the weight of her decision settle like a heavy stone on her chest.

She closed her eyes and took a deep breath, her voice steady as she whispered the only thing she knew for certain:

"I will not be consumed."

A silence fell over the clearing, and for a brief moment, the spirits paused, their eyes flickering as they regarded her. The wind shifted, the trees seemed to lean in closer, and Kaelen's gaze locked onto hers, unreadable, yet knowing.

The trial had begun.

Six

The Silent Guardian

The moon hung low in the sky, its pale light casting long, twisted shadows across the forest floor. The air was thick with the scent of damp earth and decaying leaves, the remnants of autumn's reign now forgotten beneath the encroaching weight of winter. The forest, once alive with the vibrant whispers of nature, had grown eerily still. The only sound was the occasional rustle of a leaf falling from a high branch, drifting softly to the ground, as if the world was holding its breath.

Lyra stood at the edge of the forest, her heart pounding in her chest as she watched the towering silhouette of the ancient temple ahead of her. Its stone walls rose like a jagged wound against the night sky, the once-grand structure now crumbling with the passage of time. Faint, flickering lights flickered within the cracks of the broken walls—strange, unearthly flames that

The Silent Guardian

seemed to have a life of their own.

The moment her foot stepped beyond the threshold of the forest, she felt it—a prickling sensation at the back of her neck, a subtle shift in the atmosphere that tugged at the very core of her being. She had never seen this place before, yet it felt... familiar. As though it had been waiting for her, calling to her in her dreams, pulling her toward it with invisible hands.

The pact she had made with Kaelen had marked her in ways she couldn't fully comprehend, and the pull toward this place—toward whatever secret it held—had only grown stronger with each passing day. The whispering voices had not ceased since that night in the Forest of Echoes. They continued to haunt her, always lurking just beyond the edges of her awareness, teasing her with fragments of words she couldn't quite grasp.

But tonight, as the moonlight bathed the temple in an ethereal glow, she felt a new urgency—something pulling her forward, compelling her to uncover the truth buried within these ancient stones.

Her boots crunched softly against the frost-bitten ground as she approached the entrance of the temple. The massive stone doors loomed before her, their surface engraved with intricate symbols that seemed to pulse with a faint, otherworldly light. For a moment, she hesitated, her hand hovering above the door as a wave of doubt washed over her.

What if she was making a mistake? What if the darkness that had begun to coil within her was not something she could control? She had already made a pact—one that had irrevocably bound her to Kaelen, to the forces of shadow—but this… this felt different. This temple was not simply a place of power; it was a place of knowledge, of secrets long forgotten by the living.

But before she could retreat, the door creaked open of its own accord, as though it had been waiting for her touch. The sound reverberated through the stillness, sending a shiver down her spine. Lyra stepped forward, her breath shallow, and entered the temple.

Inside, the air was cold and dry, and the flickering lights she had seen from the outside were brighter now, casting eerie shadows on the walls. The room was vast—bigger than she had expected—and filled with ancient stone pillars that rose toward the ceiling, their surfaces covered in centuries-old inscriptions. The walls were lined with faded tapestries, their once-vibrant colors now muted and faded by time.

At the far end of the chamber, a massive stone altar stood in the center of the room, its surface adorned with strange runes and symbols. It seemed to pulse with an energy of its own, a quiet hum that resonated deep within her bones. Lyra felt the familiar pull toward it, an invisible thread weaving its way into her chest, tugging her closer.

And then, she saw him.

A figure stood before the altar, cloaked in shadows. His back was turned, and he was entirely still, as if waiting for her arrival.

The Silent Guardian

The figure was tall, his form looming in the dim light. His face was hidden beneath the hood of his cloak, but even from this distance, Lyra could feel the weight of his presence. He was no ordinary man. She could sense the ancient power that radiated from him, an energy that seemed to drown out everything else in the room.

Lyra's breath caught in her throat, and her pulse quickened as she took a hesitant step forward. Her instincts screamed at her to leave, to turn and run as far away from this place as possible. But her feet moved on their own accord, her body drawn to the figure as if it had already made the decision for her.

"Who are you?" she called, her voice shaking slightly, but the words rang out in the cavernous space, reverberating off the stone walls.

The figure turned slowly, his hooded gaze settling on her with a calm intensity. His eyes were dark, almost black, and they seemed to pierce through her, as if he could see every thought, every secret she had ever tried to hide.

"You shouldn't have come here, Lyra," the figure said, his voice low and resonant, like the sound of stone grinding against stone. There was an ancient quality to his tone, as though he spoke from a time long past, from a place far beyond her understanding.

Lyra's heart raced as she tried to steady her breath. "Who are you?" she repeated, this time with more force. "What is this place?"

The figure regarded her for a moment, his expression unreadable. Then, without a word, he raised a hand, and the altar behind him flared to life with a sudden burst of light. The symbols on its surface began to glow, the runes shifting and changing, rearranging themselves into a new pattern that Lyra couldn't decipher.

"This is the heart of the temple," the figure said, his voice growing softer, more distant. "The place where the past and the present meet. The place where secrets are kept—secrets that should never have been forgotten."

He stepped closer to her, his movement fluid and silent, as though he were part of the shadows themselves. Lyra instinctively took a step back, her pulse hammering in her ears.

"The darkness you have embraced is only part of what you are," the figure continued, his voice now laced with a hint of something like sorrow. "The light that still resides within you will fight to escape, to break free from the chains you've wrapped around it. But the power of the pact, the power of the shadows, will always pull you back."

"Why are you telling me this?" Lyra demanded, her voice tinged with frustration. "Who are you to speak of my fate?"

The figure paused, his gaze locking onto hers. "I am the Guardian," he said quietly. "The keeper of these secrets. And I have watched you since you first entered the forest. I have seen the mark upon you, the bond that has been forged."

The Silent Guardian

Lyra's breath caught. "What do you mean, the bond?"

The Guardian's eyes seemed to darken, the shadows around him deepening. "The pact you made with Kaelen binds you to this place, to the power that lies dormant in the heart of the temple. But it also binds you to me, whether you wish it or not. I have been waiting for someone like you—for the one who could awaken the power that has long been dormant."

"What power?" Lyra asked, her voice barely a whisper, her heart thudding in her chest.

The Guardian's lips curled into a faint smile, though it was devoid of warmth. "The power of the dawn and the night. The power that will reshape the world, if you can learn to control it."

A sudden, deep rumble shook the ground beneath her feet, sending a jolt of fear through her. The symbols on the altar flared brighter, and the walls of the temple groaned in response, as though the very foundations of the place were awakening. The air was thick with energy, and Lyra could feel it—pulsing in her veins, crawling beneath her skin. The darkness and light inside her were fighting, struggling to break free.

"This is only the beginning, Lyra," the Guardian said, his voice barely audible above the rising hum. "The path you have chosen will not be an easy one. The power you seek will either consume you or save you. But one thing is certain—you cannot walk away from it now."

The Nightborn Prince and the Dawn Touched Maiden

Lyra's breath came in ragged gasps, her mind racing with the weight of his words. The bond with Kaelen, the darkness that now lived inside her, and the power that had been awakened in this very temple—it was all connected. She had made a choice, and there was no turning back.

The Guardian raised a hand, his fingers brushing the air as if weaving an invisible thread. "The trial has begun, Lyra. You must face the power within you, or it will consume you entirely."

The ground trembled once more, and in the distance, a loud crack echoed through the temple, followed by a low, guttural growl. The shadows around her deepened, closing in as though they had become a living thing, a force that would not let her escape.

Lyra braced herself, knowing that this was just the beginning.

Seven

The Breaking Dawn

The darkness pressed in around Lyra, wrapping itself tightly around her like an iron vice. The temple walls seemed to close in on her, the ancient stones groaning in protest, as if they, too, were waking from a long slumber. The shadows swirled at the edges of her vision, stretching toward her like dark fingers, seeking to pull her under.

Her pulse was pounding in her ears, but there was no escape from the power building within her. The pact she had made with Kaelen—the bond that now tethered her to both light and shadow—was pulsing through her veins, filling her with an overwhelming sense of both dread and purpose. Her breathing was shallow, and the weight of the decision she had made felt heavier now than it ever had before.

The altar at the center of the room hummed with energy, the

ancient runes carved into its surface glowing brighter as the ground beneath her feet began to tremble. The Guardian had spoken of the trial, but what did it mean? How was she supposed to face this power inside her when she could hardly control the force building within her chest?

She glanced around, her eyes frantically searching for some sign of what she needed to do, but the temple was silent, its shadows pressing closer with each passing second. The Guardian had vanished, leaving her alone with the rising storm of power inside her.

And then, the air shifted.

It was subtle at first, like the faintest brush of a cold wind against her skin. But it was enough to make her stop. Lyra turned slowly, her heart skipping a beat as a figure stepped from the shadows.

Kaelen.

His presence was overwhelming, suffusing the room with a sense of inevitability, as though the world had folded itself around him. His eyes—those cold, unyielding eyes—locked onto hers, and for a moment, Lyra felt the pull of his gaze, like a thread drawing her toward him.

"Lyra," he said, his voice low and smooth, like the rustle of silk. "You've done well to come this far."

She opened her mouth to speak, but no words came. She had no

The Breaking Dawn

idea what she was supposed to say. The room felt too small now, the air too thick, and she could feel the power within her rising to the surface. It was as if it had a will of its own, responding to Kaelen's presence.

"You feel it, don't you?" Kaelen asked, his voice barely above a whisper. "The pull, the hunger? The need to unleash everything that has been waiting inside you."

Lyra didn't answer, but the way her breath quickened was enough to confirm what he already knew. The power within her was no longer just a sensation—it was becoming a force, one she could hardly contain. The darkness was rising, seeping into her very bones, and the light—shimmering, faint, but there—was fighting back, unwilling to fade into nothingness.

Kaelen stepped closer, his shadow swallowing her whole as he came to stand beside her. His presence was suffocating, and yet, she couldn't pull away. The connection between them was undeniable, and for the first time, Lyra realized how deeply entwined their fates had become.

"This is where it begins," Kaelen continued, his voice reverberating through the space, sending a tremor down her spine. "The breaking dawn. You will either emerge as the one who can master both light and dark, or you will be consumed by the forces that have waited for you. You are the key, Lyra. You were always meant to carry the burden, and now, you must learn how to wield the power that flows through you."

The words made her head spin. Was this the moment? Was this

the trial? To choose between the darkness and the light? She couldn't answer that, not yet. Her body trembled with the effort to keep the power under control, to prevent it from ripping her apart.

"I don't want this," Lyra finally managed, her voice raw with emotion. "I didn't ask for this power. I didn't ask for any of it."

Kaelen's gaze softened for just a moment, but the darkness in his eyes remained, unreadable. "None of us ask for it, Lyra," he said quietly. "But it's what we are given. The question is what we do with it."

A sharp crack of thunder suddenly split the air, the sound so loud and violent it shook the very foundations of the temple. Lyra's heart skipped a beat as the shadows around her seemed to writhe in response to the storm outside. The air grew thick with energy, the tension nearly unbearable.

And then, without warning, a brilliant burst of light erupted from the altar.

Lyra stumbled back, her hands raised instinctively to shield her eyes from the blinding flare. The light seemed to pulse with an otherworldly intensity, bathing the room in its brilliance. But as her eyes adjusted, she saw something moving within the light. Shapes. Figures. Shadows.

The spirits from the forest—the ones who had watched her, tested her—were here.

They were circling the altar, their ethereal forms shimmering in the light, their eyes fixed on Lyra. She could feel their gaze, sharp and unblinking, as though they were judging her every move.

"Are you ready?" Kaelen's voice broke through the chaos, cold and cutting. "Are you ready to make your choice?"

Lyra's heart slammed against her ribcage. The light and the darkness were clashing within her, the forces pulling her in opposite directions. The spirits watched her with the weight of centuries behind their gaze, as if they were waiting for her to decide—waiting for her to embrace the truth of who she was.

She closed her eyes, breathing in deeply, trying to center herself amid the storm of conflicting emotions. The power, the rage, the fear—it was all there, surging through her. But beneath it all, there was something else. A deep, quiet thread of something pure. The light that had always existed within her, the part of herself she had feared to acknowledge, now called to her like a distant star.

But the darkness…

The darkness was seductive, overwhelming, and it whispered promises of power. Of freedom. Of control. It pulled at her, making her heart ache with the need to give in. But there was a part of her—the part that was still Lyra—that wanted to fight. That wanted to hold on to the light.

Her breath caught in her throat as the spirits closed in around her, their forms flickering like flames in the wind. The air was thick with tension, the very essence of the temple crackling with energy. This was it—the moment of reckoning.

The voices of the spirits reached her, a low murmur that filled the space like the rustling of leaves in a storm.

Choose. Choose.

"Lyra," Kaelen's voice was a soft, dangerous whisper, his breath hot against her ear. "It is time. Embrace the darkness, and you will have everything you ever wanted. You will no longer be bound by the world's rules. You will be free."

But Lyra knew. She knew deep down that freedom was not what he was offering. It was a lie. A seductive lie that would consume her. If she gave in, if she let herself fall into the shadows, she would lose herself forever.

She forced herself to take a step forward, her heart thundering in her chest. The darkness pushed against her, suffocating, but she held her ground. She would not let it win. Not without a fight.

With one final, defiant breath, Lyra closed her eyes and reached for the light inside her. She could feel it now, its warmth growing stronger with every beat of her heart. The light was fragile, but it was real.

As her fingers brushed the air before her, the light surged, exploding in a burst of energy that pushed the darkness back.

The Breaking Dawn

The spirits howled as the power within her shifted, growing stronger. The altar's glow intensified, and the temple's very walls seemed to tremble under the weight of her decision.

The breaking dawn had arrived.

Lyra opened her eyes, and for the first time since she had entered this place, she felt whole. The darkness had not consumed her. The light had not been extinguished. She had chosen. She had embraced the truth of who she was.

And now, with the power of both light and dark within her, she would face whatever came next.

The storm outside began to die down, and the first rays of dawn pierced the temple's stone walls, casting a golden light across the altar.

The trial was over.

But the journey had only just begun.

Eight

The Betrayal of the Silver King

The world seemed to warp around Lyra as she stepped out of the temple. The glow of dawn had faded into the gray mist of early morning, the sky a muted blend of colors as the sun struggled to rise above the horizon. She could still feel the remnants of the power that had surged within her, thrumming beneath her skin like a living thing, refusing to be silenced. The choice she had made, the decision to embrace both the light and the darkness, was not one she could undo. And the weight of it was heavier than she had anticipated.

Her chest ached as she pressed her hand against her heart, as if she could hold the dual forces within her in check. But it wasn't that simple. The power was there, constantly tugging at her, pulling her in two directions at once.

She had chosen, and now the consequences were becoming all

too real.

As she made her way through the temple grounds, the weight of the moment pressing on her every step, she heard the unmistakable sound of hooves behind her. Her heart skipped a beat. A chill crept down her spine as she turned toward the sound, her instincts screaming that something was wrong. The air had grown colder, heavier, and the once peaceful surroundings now seemed ominous.

A figure emerged from the mist, his silhouette dark against the pale backdrop of the forest. Lyra's breath caught in her throat as the rider came into full view.

The Silver King.

His steed was a massive, black warhorse, its coat gleaming like polished obsidian, its eyes glowing faintly in the morning light. The King himself was tall, clad in silver armor that shimmered unnaturally in the dim light. His face was partially obscured by a silver mask, but his piercing, ice-blue eyes were unmistakable. They locked onto Lyra with a hunger she had not expected.

The Silver King had always been a figure of whispered legends—a ruler who controlled vast lands and wielded power over both life and death. But Lyra had never truly understood the extent of his reach, or the darkness that lay beneath the surface of his princely exterior.

She had heard stories. Stories of how his charm and charisma could bend entire armies to his will. Of how he had once been a noble ruler, respected by all. But now? Now, he was nothing more than a shadow of the past, his hunger for power growing insatiable.

"What are you doing here?" Lyra demanded, her voice steady but her pulse quickening with every breath.

The Silver King dismounted, his movements slow and deliberate, as though he were savoring the moment. He stood tall before her, his presence suffocating, his eyes cold as ice. For a moment, neither spoke, the only sound the distant rustling of the trees. The air felt thick with tension, as if something was on the verge of breaking.

"I came for you, Lyra," the Silver King said, his voice smooth, like the hum of steel on stone. "I've been watching you. Watching your every move."

Lyra's stomach tightened. "What do you want from me?" she demanded, taking a step back. The connection between her and Kaelen, the strange bond of light and dark, was still fresh in her mind, and she could feel the stirrings of it deep within her chest. She could feel the shadows calling to her, and she knew they would answer if she let them.

The Silver King stepped closer, his gaze never leaving hers. "You are more powerful than you realize, Lyra. More than I ever imagined. And that power... it belongs to me."

A chill ran through her at his words, and she forced herself to stand tall, though every instinct in her screamed to run. "You

The Betrayal of the Silver King

have no claim over me," she said, her voice sharp. "I made a pact. I chose my path."

He smiled, though the expression didn't reach his eyes. "Ah, yes. The pact. With Kaelen." His voice dripped with disdain as he spoke the name. "You think that makes you untouchable? That the shadows will protect you? But you are just a pawn, Lyra. A pawn in a much larger game."

Her heart skipped a beat as his words sank in. What did he mean? What game was he talking about?

"I've known for some time now that you would come here," he continued, his tone mocking, as though she were a child to be scolded. "I've watched you, and I've watched Kaelen. And I've known the truth all along. The power you've awakened… it isn't just Kaelen's to control. It's mine."

A flood of realization washed over her, and she felt her breath catch in her throat. The Silver King wasn't here by chance. He had known about her, about the pact, and about Kaelen from the very beginning. He had been playing a far more dangerous game than she had imagined, and she had been nothing more than a piece on his board.

The Silver King stepped even closer, his voice dropping to a low, dangerous whisper. "You see, Lyra, the pact you made wasn't just with Kaelen. It was with me, too. I've been waiting for this moment—for the moment when you would come into your full power. And now that you have, you will help me take what is rightfully mine."

The ground beneath her seemed to shift, and her stomach twisted with a sickening realization. The darkness she had embraced was not just Kaelen's power—it was a power that the Silver King had been coveting for years, and she had unwittingly stepped into his trap.

"You lied to me," Lyra breathed, the words barely escaping her lips. The betrayal stung, sharper than any blade. The Silver King had been playing both sides—using her to further his own ends, manipulating her into believing that she was making her own choices, when in reality, he had been the one pulling the strings all along.

The Silver King's smile widened. "Of course I lied," he said, his voice cold and detached. "You never truly thought you were in control, did you? You think you have the power to defy the darkness, but you were always meant to serve it. And now, with you at my side, we can reshape the world as it was meant to be. No more pretending. No more false kings. It will be my rule. Forever."

Lyra's blood ran cold as his words echoed in her mind. She could feel the power inside her stirring, but it was no longer something she could trust. The darkness she had embraced had always been dangerous, but now it felt like a looming storm, threatening to swallow her whole.

"No," she whispered, shaking her head. "I will never help you. I've made my choice, and I won't let you turn me into your puppet."

The Betrayal of the Silver King

The Silver King's eyes narrowed, and for a brief moment, something dark flickered behind his mask. "You don't have a choice, Lyra," he said, his voice low and threatening. "You are already mine. Whether you accept it or not."

Before she could respond, the ground beneath them trembled, the temple's stones groaning in protest. The shadows around them seemed to shift, moving in unnatural patterns as if they were alive. Lyra felt a surge of energy—a force that was both cold and suffocating—rising from the depths of the earth. It was the Silver King's power, and it was flooding into her, binding her to him.

She gasped as the darkness coiled around her like a serpent, tightening its grip. The mark on her wrist flared to life, burning with an intensity that made her knees buckle. The Silver King's laughter echoed in her ears, a sound that sent shivers down her spine.

"Welcome to your new reality, Lyra," he whispered, his voice like poison. "You belong to me now."

The world around her spun, and for a moment, she was consumed by the darkness. She could feel it—the pull of the Silver King's influence, dragging her deeper into the abyss.

But deep inside her, there was a flicker of light, a glimmer of hope. She had made her choice once before, and she could make it again. She would fight. She would not be his pawn.

She clenched her fists, the power inside her surging in response.

The Nightborn Prince and the Dawn Touched Maiden

The dawn was breaking, and Lyra would not let the shadows swallow her whole. Not now. Not ever.

With a final, defiant breath, she pushed back against the darkness, fighting with everything she had.

The Silver King's smirk faltered for a brief moment, and in that moment of weakness, Lyra made her move.

The battle had only just begun.

Nine

The Shadowed Heart

The walls of the Silver King's fortress loomed before Lyra, towering and oppressive, their cold stone facades reflecting the pale light of the waning moon. The air was thick with the scent of damp stone and the faint trace of smoke. The fortress was silent—eerily so—as if the very earth beneath it was holding its breath. There was no wind, no rustle of trees, just an overwhelming, unnatural stillness.

Lyra's heart thundered in her chest, her breath shallow and uneven as she approached the massive iron doors that marked the entrance. The weight of the Silver King's power pressed down on her from all sides, suffocating, relentless. She could feel the darkness within her, the pull of the shadows threatening to drag her under, but she had to resist. She had no choice but to keep moving forward.

The Nightborn Prince and the Dawn Touched Maiden

The betrayal had shattered her. She had believed in the Silver King's lies, had thought him a ruler of honor, someone who could restore balance to the world. But he was nothing more than a manipulator, a puppet master, using her as a pawn in his game. And she, blinded by her desperation for power, had fallen right into his trap.

But no longer. She would not let him control her. She would not become his weapon.

She placed her hand on the cold iron door, feeling the vibrations of power ripple through the metal. A deep hum, like the pulse of a beating heart, thrummed beneath her fingers. The door creaked open slowly, its massive weight groaning in protest. The dark corridors inside the fortress beckoned her forward, the shadows at their edges twisting as though alive.

With a steadying breath, Lyra stepped inside, her footsteps echoing through the vast, empty space. The torches lining the walls flickered, casting long, dancing shadows that seemed to stretch toward her like reaching fingers. Her instincts screamed at her to turn back, to escape while she still could, but she forced herself to move forward. The Silver King was close. She could feel it. And she would face him—on her terms.

As she descended deeper into the heart of the fortress, the air grew colder. The chill bit at her skin, seeping into her bones. She pressed her hand against the stone walls for support, the weight of the darkness growing heavier with each step. The whispers that had plagued her since the pact with Kaelen were louder now, their words insistent and frantic. Embrace

The Shadowed Heart

it. Embrace the power. They urged, a thousand voices rising together in a cacophony of desire.

But Lyra resisted. She would not listen to them. She would not succumb.

The hallway twisted and turned, a labyrinth of dark corridors, each one seemingly endless, until finally, she reached the heart of the fortress. The chamber before her was vast, its high ceiling lost in shadows, the air thick with an oppressive energy that made her skin crawl. In the center of the room stood a massive stone altar, its surface covered in strange, ancient symbols that seemed to pulse with a life of their own. The shadows here were thicker, darker than anywhere else in the fortress, and they pressed in on her from all sides.

And then she saw him.

The Silver King stood at the far end of the room, his figure bathed in the dim light of a flickering torch. His armor gleamed like liquid silver, reflecting the faint light in harsh, sharp angles. His face, partially obscured by his mask, was unreadable, but the coldness in his eyes was unmistakable. He was waiting for her.

Lyra's breath caught in her throat, and for a moment, she faltered. She could feel the pull of the darkness, the storm within her rising once again, urging her to submit to him. But this time, she was stronger. She had made her choice.

"I knew you would come," the Silver King said, his voice a soft rasp, like ice scraping against stone. "You're like a moth to a flame, Lyra. Always drawn to the power, to the danger. But you never understand the cost."

She gritted her teeth, her fists clenched at her sides. "You lied to me," she spat, her voice cold with fury. "You never cared about balance. You never cared about saving anyone. You just wanted control."

The Silver King's lips curled into a smile, but it was devoid of warmth. "You misunderstand me," he said, his tone almost pitying. "I am balance. I am control. Without me, everything would crumble. The world is chaos, Lyra. And I alone can fix it."

Her eyes narrowed, her hands trembling with the effort it took to suppress the power rising within her. She could feel it, the darkness that flowed like liquid fire beneath her skin, the call to unleash it, to give in to the hunger that clawed at her every thought.

"You're wrong," she said, her voice steady, though the effort to hold herself together was becoming unbearable. "What you offer isn't balance. It's destruction."

The Silver King stepped closer, his movements slow, deliberate, as though he were savoring the moment. "You think you understand power," he said, his voice low and dangerous. "But you've only just begun to scratch the surface. I can show you how to wield it. How to bend the world to your will. You can be the ruler you were always meant to be, Lyra. We can rule together."

The words hung in the air, thick with temptation. Lyra could feel the darkness swirling around her, caressing her skin, urging her to accept. The hunger in her veins grew sharper, and for a moment, she was almost overwhelmed by the power inside her. It would be so easy. So easy to give in.

But then, a flicker of light shone in the back of her mind. Kaelen's face, haunted but resolute, flashed before her eyes. The warmth of the light she had chosen—the light she had fought to keep alive within her—flickered like a distant star. The darkness could never win. She had made her choice.

"No," she whispered, her voice shaking with the effort it took to say the word. "I won't join you."

The Silver King's expression darkened, his eyes narrowing into dangerous slits. He raised his hand, and the shadows in the room seemed to thicken, closing in on Lyra, suffocating her. She could feel the weight of his power pressing down on her, the darkness curling around her like chains.

"You think you have a choice?" he hissed. "You think you can defy me? You are mine, Lyra. Your power, your soul, they belong to me."

She gasped as the darkness surged forward, wrapping around her like a vice, pulling her toward him. The power inside her screamed for release, for control, for freedom. But she pushed against it, her hands raised to ward off the darkness that threatened to swallow her whole.

"I am not yours!" she shouted, her voice echoing in the chamber, raw with defiance.

The Silver King's laugh was like ice cracking. "You are foolish to fight it. The more you resist, the stronger it becomes."

His words rang true. Lyra could feel the darkness closing in, the weight of the shadows pressing on her chest, suffocating her. Her vision blurred, and the whispers returned, louder now, frantic and desperate.

Embrace it. Let go.

The storm inside her raged, but Lyra closed her eyes, drawing on the light within her, the warmth she had fought so hard to protect. She would not let the darkness win. She would not let the Silver King break her.

With a cry of determination, she let the light surge outward, pushing against the shadows with every ounce of strength she had. The darkness screamed in protest, but the light burned, searing through the shadows like the dawn breaking through the night.

The Silver King staggered back, his mask falling slightly, revealing the anger and frustration on his face. He raised his hands, his power surging toward her, but Lyra held firm, the light within her a shield against his assault.

"You cannot defeat me," he snarled, his eyes blazing with fury.

But Lyra, shaking with exhaustion but resolute in her defiance, met his gaze. "I already have."

The Silver King's fury was palpable, but for the first time, Lyra felt the balance shift. The power that had once threatened to overwhelm her now surged with purpose. She would not be his pawn. She would not bow to his darkness.

And in that moment, she knew: the battle for her soul was far from over.

But she would fight to the end.

Ten

The Dance of Light and Dark

Lyra's breath came in shallow gasps as she stood in the center of the darkened chamber. The Silver King's presence still lingered in the air, like a storm cloud waiting to break. Her body was trembling from the battle, the light within her flickering like a candle in the wind, but she held her ground. She had resisted him once, but she knew this wasn't over. The Silver King was not a man who gave up easily, and neither was she.

The fortress, once a place of power, now seemed like a tomb—its stone walls groaning under the weight of the unseen forces that battled within. The flickering torches cast long shadows that stretched across the walls like dark fingers, reaching for her. The air was thick, suffocating, charged with the aftermath of the confrontation. The power between them had clashed, and now the world around her seemed to hold its breath.

The Dance of Light and Dark

Her heart was racing, her pulse thumping loudly in her ears, but Lyra couldn't afford to falter. The Silver King might have been momentarily repelled, but she could feel the weight of his anger. She could feel his eyes on her, even now, as though he were lurking just beyond the shadows, waiting for her to make a mistake.

She turned sharply, her boots echoing on the stone floor, and there he was. Kaelen.

His presence was unmistakable, but something about him had changed. He was no longer the figure of cold resolve she had once known; his eyes were dark, almost feverish, and there was a tension in the air around him. He looked different, somehow—more dangerous. And in that moment, Lyra couldn't tell if the fear that gnawed at her was for him or because of him.

"Kaelen?" Her voice cracked, uncertainty creeping into her tone. "What are you doing here?"

He stood motionless, just within the shadows, as if he were part of them. His eyes locked onto hers, unblinking, as though searching for something. His lips parted, but for a moment, no words came. His silence was unsettling, more so than any threat he could make. The connection between them, the bond forged by their pact, thrummed in the air, tugging at Lyra's chest.

"I never meant for it to be like this," Kaelen said, his voice low, laced with an emotion she couldn't place. His eyes darted briefly to the ground, as though the weight of his words was too much to bear. "I never wanted to drag you into this—into his game."

Lyra's chest tightened, her mind racing. "What do you mean? Who's game?"

Kaelen stepped forward, his movements slow but deliberate, like he was testing the space between them, gauging her reaction. "The Silver King. He was never who he claimed to be. I knew this was coming, but I never expected him to play you against me."

Her heart sank as his words settled over her. She had known that something was off—that the Silver King was a dangerous manipulator—but now, hearing Kaelen speak of him like this, she realized just how deep the deception ran. She had been pulled into something far darker than she had ever imagined.

"You said you were going to help me," she whispered, her voice strained. "You said you weren't like him."

Kaelen's eyes flashed, a flicker of something painful crossing his features. "I never lied to you. Not about that. But I never told you everything." His eyes burned with an intensity that made her feel small, like he was seeing something within her that she hadn't even realized was there. "He's been playing both sides all along, Lyra. And now he wants you. He wants you."

The words hit her like a physical blow. Her mind reeled, trying to process everything. The Silver King's betrayal had been bad enough, but the idea that Kaelen had been hiding things from her—it felt like a betrayal of its own. She had trusted him. She had believed in him. But now, doubt crept in like poison, clouding her thoughts.

The Dance of Light and Dark

"Why didn't you tell me this sooner?" she asked, her voice breaking. "Why didn't you warn me?"

"I couldn't," Kaelen answered, his voice softening, filled with regret. "You were already in too deep. The moment you made the pact, it was no longer just about you and me. The Silver King was always watching, always pulling the strings. I couldn't protect you from him, not fully, not without making things worse."

Lyra took a step back, the weight of his words sinking in. Her stomach twisted with a mixture of betrayal and confusion. She had trusted Kaelen, but she didn't know who he was anymore—or who she was, for that matter.

"Then what now?" she demanded, her voice shaking with a mix of anger and fear. "What do you want from me now?"

For the first time, Kaelen's expression shifted, his eyes darkening with a resolve that made Lyra's heart skip a beat. "I want you to choose."

Her breath caught in her throat. "Choose what?"

"Choose the path you take from here," he said, his voice low and tense. "The Silver King's grip is tightening around you, Lyra. And now that you've tasted both the light and the dark, you need to decide which side you'll stand on. Because if you don't, you will be lost."

The tension in the room escalated, the power crackling in the

The Nightborn Prince and the Dawn Touched Maiden

air between them. Lyra could feel it, could feel the pull of the darkness inside her, beckoning her to embrace it, to give in to its seductive promise of power. She could feel the light within her, too, flickering weakly, struggling against the storm of shadows that threatened to overwhelm it.

Kaelen stepped closer, his voice dropping to a whisper. "You're stronger than you realize. But you have to decide. The Silver King will stop at nothing to have you. To break you. And you're the only one who can stop him."

Lyra's mind spun, the weight of the decision pressing down on her like an invisible hand. She had made her choice once before—she had embraced both the light and the dark, bound herself to the forces that were beyond her control. But now, faced with the raw, crushing reality of the Silver King's power, she had to ask herself: Was she strong enough to wield both without being consumed by them?

Kaelen's gaze never wavered, his eyes locked on hers, as if searching for the answer within her. The tension between them was thick, as though the very air around them was pulsing with the power of their choices.

Lyra swallowed hard, her pulse racing, and for a moment, it felt like the world stood still, waiting for her to make her move. She could feel the darkness closing in, could feel the weight of the power she held, and she realized, for the first time, that her decision was not just about her—it was about the fate of everything around her.

The Dance of Light and Dark

"I'm not your weapon," she said finally, her voice firm, though her chest felt tight with the effort it took to say the words. "I won't be controlled. Not by you. Not by him."

Kaelen's eyes flashed with something like surprise, but then his expression hardened, as though he had known this would come. "Then the battle is yours to fight, Lyra," he said quietly. "But know this—whatever you decide, the consequences will be far-reaching."

Lyra's heart was racing, but her resolve solidified. She was no one's pawn. She would not let herself be dragged into the darkness, no matter how tempting it was. She had a choice. And it was time to make it.

She stepped forward, her eyes locked on Kaelen's, and she said, with a quiet certainty, "I choose the light."

The shadows in the room seemed to recoil, as if they were wounded by her words, but the light within her flared brighter, burning against the encroaching darkness. It was a fleeting victory, but it was hers. For now.

Kaelen's gaze softened for just a moment, but then he stepped back, his expression unreadable. "The game is far from over, Lyra. But for now… it's your move."

The dance between light and dark had only just begun.

Eleven

The Heart of Betrayal

The silence that followed the Silver King's fall was deafening. The walls of the throne room, once alive with the echoes of power and authority, now stood still, as if the very stones were exhausted from bearing the weight of the deceit and manipulation that had stained them. Lyra stood alone in the center of the room, her chest heaving as the last remnants of her power flickered out. The light she had wielded with such intensity faded, leaving her in the cold, oppressive darkness of the aftermath.

The Silver King lay at her feet, his once-unyielding form now crumpled and broken, a shadow of the man he had been. His eyes, wide with shock and disbelief, were fixed on her, but there was no longer any defiance there—only a hollow emptiness.

The air in the room was thick with the scent of burned wood

The Heart of Betrayal

and the faint remnants of dark magic. The power that had surged so violently through her veins now seemed to dissipate, leaving a void in its wake. Lyra felt the emptiness in her chest, the quiet ache of something lost. It wasn't just the Silver King's defeat that had left her feeling hollow—it was the weight of the choices she had made, the price she had paid.

Her heart still raced, but there was a new fear gnawing at her. The silence was heavy, oppressive, as if the world itself was holding its breath, waiting for something—waiting for her to make the next move.

She stepped closer to the fallen King, the sound of her boots clicking against the stone floor like the ticking of a clock. Her eyes never left him. She had fought for this moment. She had fought for the light to shine through the darkness, but now, standing over the Silver King's broken form, she wasn't sure what victory really meant.

"I should have known," she whispered to herself, her voice trembling with exhaustion. "I should have seen it coming."

She had seen the signs. She had felt the weight of the Silver King's manipulation in every interaction, in every whisper that slipped between their words. His lies had been too convincing, his promises too sweet. He had played her, just as he had played everyone else.

But there was something more—a deeper betrayal she had yet to fully understand.

As she turned away from the King's fallen form, the air around her grew colder, the shadows creeping in once again. A whisper in the darkness tugged at the edges of her thoughts, like a spider weaving a thread of doubt.

She had broken free of the Silver King's grasp, but at what cost?

Suddenly, the ground beneath her feet trembled, a low rumble vibrating through the floor like the warning of an approaching storm. Lyra's heart skipped a beat as the shadows in the corners of the room seemed to grow darker, more alive, as if they were converging on her from all sides.

The whispers grew louder.

You cannot escape it.

Her breath quickened, panic rising in her chest. The power she had released in the throne room had not just severed the Silver King's hold over her—it had opened something else. The magic, the darkness, had been waiting for this moment, and now it sought to claim her. The very air around her seemed to pulse with that hunger.

Lyra spun around, her pulse racing, her body tense. The shadows were moving, alive, swirling with an almost malevolent intent. They reached toward her, grasping, pulling at her, as though they recognized her weakness.

No.

She would not let it claim her. She had fought too hard, had bled too much, to fall now.

But the darkness pressed against her with a force that she could not deny. She felt the sharp sting of the magic wrapping around her once more, like cold fingers digging into her flesh. Her breath came in ragged gasps as she fought to hold it back, to keep the darkness at bay.

The shadows crept closer, now taking shape, forming into something solid, something more dangerous. And then, from the depths of the room, a figure emerged from the darkness.

Kaelen.

Lyra's heart clenched at the sight of him, but there was no warmth in his gaze. His once familiar expression had hardened, his eyes now cold and calculating. The shadows that clung to him seemed to writhe with a life of their own, swirling around him like a cloak, as if they were part of him.

"You..." Lyra breathed, her voice barely above a whisper. "What are you doing here?"

Kaelen didn't answer immediately. He stepped closer, his every movement deliberate, as if the very space between them was charged with something far more dangerous than the darkness itself. The air seemed to crackle with tension, and Lyra's chest tightened.

"I thought you were dead," she said, her voice shaking with a mix of confusion and betrayal. "I thought you were gone."

"I was," Kaelen replied, his voice soft, almost detached. "But I never truly left."

He reached out a hand, the shadows shifting in response, curling around his fingers like they were alive. "I've been waiting for you, Lyra. Waiting for the moment when you would finally make your choice."

Lyra's heart sank as she looked at him, her thoughts a whirlwind of confusion and anger. The betrayal from the Silver King had stung deeply, but this—this felt worse. This was not just another twist in a game. This was Kaelen, standing before her, wielding the very darkness she had fought against.

"You were playing me all along," she said, her voice cold with fury. "From the beginning."

Kaelen's gaze flickered with something like regret, but it was fleeting. "No, Lyra. I was protecting you. But the power you hold—both light and dark—it has always been too dangerous. I never wanted to see you fall under its weight."

"You didn't want me to fall?" Lyra's laugh was bitter, sharp. "You were using me just like he was."

Kaelen flinched at her words, but his resolve did not falter. "I did what I had to do. You had to see it for yourself. The truth is more complicated than either of us realized."

The Heart of Betrayal

Lyra took a step back, her heart pounding as the shadows seemed to close in on her. "What truth, Kaelen? What are you trying to tell me?"

"The Silver King was never the true threat," Kaelen said, his voice low, his eyes dark with something unreadable. "The true enemy was always the power—the power inside you. The light and dark were never meant to coexist. And the moment you embraced both, you set the stage for everything to unravel."

Lyra's mind raced. His words, though soft, hit her like a hammer to the chest. She had chosen to wield both the light and the dark, but now she saw—Kaelen had never been on her side. He had been protecting her from the truth, from herself.

"I didn't ask for this," Lyra whispered, her voice breaking. "I didn't ask for any of this."

The shadows surrounding them shifted, swirling with a life of their own. The very air seemed to hum with tension, the room growing darker by the second. The walls themselves seemed to lean inward, as if closing in on them, trapping them in this moment.

Kaelen took a step forward, his eyes softening. "Lyra, you don't understand. I'm trying to protect you. From yourself. The power you possess—it isn't something that can simply be controlled. It will destroy you. It will destroy everything."

The darkness pressed in closer, its grip tightening around her chest, but Lyra held her ground. She could feel it—this was the moment. The decision she had been waiting for. She had been running from the truth, from Kaelen, from the power inside her, but now it was time to face it.

With a cry of defiance, she stepped forward, shoving the darkness back with every ounce of strength she could muster. The power within her flared to life, a fierce light that burned through the shadows.

Kaelen's expression flickered with something close to fear as the darkness writhed around him, fighting against the light. "You can't do this, Lyra," he said, his voice laced with desperation.

"I can," she replied, her voice strong, unwavering. "And I will."

In that moment, as the shadows fought the light, Lyra knew—this battle was far from over. But she had made her choice. She would not let the darkness consume her. And Kaelen? He would have to choose, too.

The room trembled, and the battle between light and dark raged on, threatening to tear everything apart. But Lyra stood, resolute, the power within her now a weapon, a shield, and a promise.

The world was changing, and she would be the one to decide what came next.

Twelve

The Shattered Oath

The storm had come suddenly, but its fury had never let up. The sky was blackened, thunder rolling in the distance, and the winds whipped through the desolate landscape like the breath of a vengeful god. Lyra stood at the edge of the Silver King's fortress, staring out into the chaos of the night. The storm mirrored the turmoil inside her—raging, wild, and untamable. Her chest ached with the weight of what had happened, what was still to come.

The echoes of Kaelen's words lingered in her mind. *You can't escape what you are, Lyra. You've already made your choice. And that choice is going to tear us both apart.*

She didn't know if she could fight that truth. She had chosen once before, when she had embraced both the light and the dark, but now she was lost in the space between them. The battle had shifted in ways she could never have predicted, and she was no longer sure where the light ended and the darkness began. But one thing was certain—Kaelen's betrayal had opened her eyes. He had been her guide, her mentor, her tether to a world she didn't fully understand. But now, the man who had once claimed to protect her had become part of the problem.

Her hand trembled as she reached for the stone wall of the fortress, leaning against it for support. She couldn't escape it, the power inside her. The darkness gnawed at the edges of her mind, whispering promises of strength, of control, of an end to the chaos. It was tempting, too tempting to resist. But Lyra had learned that the price of embracing it was more than she was willing to pay.

The storm raged louder now, the wind howling like a wild beast in the distance. She couldn't stay here, not in this place of broken promises and shattered alliances. There was something she needed to find, something she had to understand about the power that had been awakened within her. It was time to face what had been hiding in the shadows, to seek the truth that Kaelen had tried to protect her from.

Her breath caught as a shadow moved at the corner of her vision. For a moment, she thought it was just the storm, a trick of the wind or the flickering torches in the distance. But then the figure emerged from the darkness, stepping into the dim light of the fortress.

It was him.

The Shattered Oath

The figure was tall, draped in a cloak of shadows, his movements fluid and almost predatory. His face was partially obscured by a hood, but his eyes gleamed with an unsettling intensity. Lyra's heart skipped a beat, her instincts screaming at her to run. But there was no escape now. Not from him.

"Kaelen," she whispered, her voice catching in her throat. "Why are you here?"

He didn't answer immediately, his gaze sweeping over her with a hunger that sent a chill crawling up her spine. His presence was like a storm of its own, pushing against her in ways she didn't understand. The shadows seemed to pulse around him, alive and eager.

"I never wanted this," Kaelen finally said, his voice low and gravelly. "I never wanted to be the one to tear everything apart. But you, Lyra... you've become more powerful than I ever imagined."

Her heart pounded in her chest as she stepped back, keeping her distance. "More powerful?" she echoed, her voice trembling. "What do you mean? I'm losing myself, Kaelen. This—this power—it's tearing me apart. And you... you're not the one who's been honest with me."

Kaelen's eyes darkened, his expression unreadable. "I did what I had to do. You were never meant to face this alone. You were never meant to face what's inside you. The power you've embraced—it's not something that can be controlled. It will break you, Lyra. It will break everything."

His words struck deep, each one resonating within her like a cold stone sinking into her chest. She could feel it, the darkness clawing at her, pushing her to give in, to let go of the light. She could feel the pull of it—the seductive promises of control, of power. She had tasted it before, felt its temptation. But now, she could sense the danger in it, the cost.

She swallowed hard, trying to steady her breath. "Then why didn't you warn me?" she asked, her voice breaking. "Why didn't you tell me the truth?"

Kaelen's jaw clenched, and for a moment, the shadows around him seemed to grow heavier, more oppressive. "Because I thought you could handle it. I thought I could protect you. But now... I've seen what you've become, and it terrifies me."

Lyra shook her head, tears welling in her eyes, though she refused to let them fall. "You were supposed to be my protector," she whispered. "But you've been hiding the truth from me this entire time. All along, you were keeping me in the dark, hoping I wouldn't see who you really are."

Kaelen's face twisted in frustration. "You don't understand. I had no choice! The darkness inside you—inside us—has always been part of the plan. It's what we are. It's what we've always been."

Lyra's breath caught in her throat, her mind racing as she tried to piece the fragments together. "Part of the plan?" she asked, the words tasting like ash on her tongue. "Whose plan? What do you mean?"

The Shattered Oath

For a moment, Kaelen was silent, his eyes never leaving hers. The weight of his gaze felt like an anchor, pulling her deeper into the storm that raged inside her.

"The Silver King wasn't the only one who wanted control," Kaelen said, his voice softer now, almost resigned. "He wasn't the only one who saw you as a tool. You've been part of a much larger game, Lyra. A game that's been played for centuries. The pact, the power… it's all connected. And you were always meant to be the fulcrum—the pivot point between light and dark."

Lyra felt as though the ground had shifted beneath her. The world she had fought to protect—the world she had thought she was saving—was not what it seemed. The shadows inside her, the power she had feared and embraced, had always been part of something bigger, something she didn't understand.

She staggered back, her hands trembling. "So, I've been nothing more than a pawn," she whispered, the words tasting bitter. "A tool in your game."

Kaelen's face softened, his expression full of regret. "No," he said, taking a step toward her. "You were never just a pawn. You were always more. But the game… it's bigger than us. We've both been caught in it. The choice is no longer ours to make. It's the only choice left, Lyra. We either accept what we are, or we're destroyed by it."

A silence hung heavy in the air between them, the storm outside raging louder than ever. Lyra's heart was beating so loudly in her chest, she couldn't think. Her hands clenched into fists, but the conflict inside her raged, pulling her in opposite directions. She had spent so long believing in the fight between light and dark, that she had never stopped to wonder if there was a third path—if there was a way out of the game entirely.

But the storm had come, and the game was about to change. Her power, both a gift and a curse, was reaching its climax. And with it, the world itself seemed to hold its breath, waiting for her to choose.

The darkness whispered again. You can wield it. You can break free. You can take control.

But the light flickered in her heart, as fragile as it had always been. There is another way.

And as the storm outside reached its crescendo, Lyra understood one thing: the game was not over. The choice had always been hers.

And now, the time had come to shatter the oath she had made.

Thirteen

The Betrayer's Blade

The sky above was a bruised canvas of violet and crimson, a storm churning in the heavens as though the world itself was at war. Thunder cracked with deafening force, the sound shaking the very ground beneath Lyra's feet. She stood at the edge of the ravine, the abyss yawning before her, its darkness seemingly endless. The wind whipped her cloak around her, its sharp bite sinking through her skin, but she hardly noticed. Her body was numb, every step heavier than the last, each one carrying her further into the storm, further into the unknown.

In the distance, the fortress of the Silver King loomed, now a crumbling ruin bathed in a dark, foreboding light. She could still feel the remnants of the battle in her bones, the raw power that had surged through her in the wake of his fall. But now, it was different. The light she had once relied upon felt distant, fading, replaced by something far more dangerous.

The air crackled with tension as she stepped forward, her eyes scanning the horizon. She had left the remnants of the Silver King's army behind, a broken empire scattered to the wind. But one force still remained—one that would not be so easily vanquished.

Kaelen.

The memory of him—the betrayal, the lies, the manipulation—was a jagged shard lodged deep within her heart. He had promised her the truth, had led her to believe that they were fighting together. But in the end, he had only sought to control her, to use her as a pawn in a game that neither of them had been prepared for.

She could still hear his words echoing in her mind, cold and unrelenting. You were always meant to be the fulcrum—the pivot point between light and dark.

"I'll never let you control me," she had whispered in the silence of the throne room, but the words felt hollow now. She had given everything to protect the balance, to preserve the world she had known. But in the end, all that had been left was betrayal.

The wind howled again, and Lyra's gaze snapped back to the path ahead. Something was coming. She could feel it. The world was shifting, and there was no escaping the storm. She had spent so long running from the truth, from the power that had defined her, but now, there was no turning back. She had

The Betrayer's Blade

to face it. She had to face him.

A figure appeared in the distance, emerging from the fog like a ghost from the past. Lyra's breath caught in her throat as she recognized him.

Kaelen.

He was no longer the man she had once known. The shadows that clung to him were darker now, deeper, as though they had consumed him whole. His once-pristine cloak was torn, his hair disheveled, and his face—his face was harder, older, the lines of battle etched into his skin. His eyes, those eyes that had once been filled with warmth, were now cold, unforgiving.

"I knew you'd come," he said, his voice low, gravelly, and full of something that sent a shiver down her spine. "I knew you'd come for me."

Lyra swallowed, her hand instinctively resting on the hilt of her dagger. "You betrayed me, Kaelen," she said, her voice raw with anger. "You've always been playing me. You never cared about me, about us—it was always about power."

Kaelen's lips curled into a bitter smile. "Power? Is that what you think this is about?" He took a step closer, his boots crunching against the ground, the tension between them palpable. "It's always been about survival, Lyra. You and I—we were never meant to be more than weapons. Pieces on a chessboard."

"You used me," Lyra spat, her heart pounding with fury. "You manipulated me, lied to me. And for what? To get control over the power I wield?"

Kaelen's gaze softened for a moment, his eyes darkening with something like regret. "I never wanted to hurt you," he said quietly, almost to himself. "But you have no idea what you've unleashed. What we've both unleashed. The darkness—the power—it's too much for any one person to control."

"And yet, here you are," Lyra said, her voice trembling with the weight of the betrayal. "You're still trying to control it, trying to control me."

Kaelen's eyes flickered with something that could have been anger, or maybe despair. "You think I want this?" he whispered. "I wanted to protect you. I wanted to keep you safe from it. But now, it's too late. The pact, the power—it's all broken. And the world is about to burn."

Her heart clenched, but she didn't move. "You're wrong. You're just as much a part of the problem as he was. The Silver King lied to me. And so did you."

Kaelen took another step closer, his voice barely above a whisper. "I never lied to you, Lyra. I just… I just didn't tell you the truth. But you have to understand—it's too late. The darkness is already here. And I'm the only one who can control it now."

She recoiled as his words hit her like a slap. "You think you can control it?" she said, her voice rising in disbelief. "The darkness doesn't care about you, Kaelen. It never has."

Kaelen's expression hardened. "You don't understand, do you?" His hand reached out, grasping her wrist with surprising strength. "This was always meant to happen. You were never supposed to fight this alone. You were never supposed to face the consequences of your choices. But you've opened the gate, and now…"

He trailed off, his grip tightening, the shadows swirling around him, responding to his command. Lyra gasped, trying to pull away, but his hold was unyielding. The darkness around them grew, pressing in, closing the distance between them.

"No," she whispered, her heart pounding. "No, Kaelen, this isn't you."

But his eyes, his cold, empty eyes, told her everything she needed to know. "You made me this way, Lyra," he said, his voice tinged with something darker than regret. "You made me believe in something more. But now… Now, I am beyond saving."

Her pulse raced as the shadows seemed to encircle them, a suffocating darkness that clung to her, choking the light. Kaelen's power, the very thing that had once been their shared connection, was now the force that threatened to consume her.

"No, Kaelen," she gasped, struggling to break free. "This isn't what we were meant to be."

The Nightborn Prince and the Dawn Touched Maiden

But Kaelen didn't answer. His grip on her tightened as the darkness pulsed with a newfound hunger, a ravenous force that clawed at the edges of her soul. The shadows around them thickened, becoming a living thing, a manifestation of the power they had both sought to control.

And then, in a movement so fast that it took her breath away, Kaelen drew a blade—a jagged, obsidian sword that gleamed darkly in the flickering light of the storm. Lyra's eyes widened in shock as he raised it, the weight of the blade shimmering with a dangerous, final intent.

"No!" she cried, her voice shaking. "Kaelen, please..."

But there was no mercy in his eyes.

In that moment, the storm outside broke. The wind howled, the sky splitting open in a violent burst of lightning, and Kaelen's blade descended. The world seemed to slow, the air thick with impending doom.

Lyra had but an instant to react. With every ounce of strength she could muster, she wrenched herself free from his grip, her hand reaching for her own dagger. But Kaelen was faster. His blade slashed through the air like a shadow itself, and Lyra felt the sting of it, sharp and deep, as it grazed her side.

She gasped, the pain searing through her, but she didn't falter. She had no time to think, only to survive.

The battle between them was not over, not yet. But in that

instant, she realized something—Kaelen had already chosen. He had given himself over to the darkness, and now she had to decide once again: to embrace the light, or to fall with him into the abyss.

And the storm raged on, a reflection of the storm inside her.

Fourteen

The Fall of Night

The blade was an extension of Kaelen's rage, gleaming in the dim light as it sliced through the air. Lyra barely managed to block it, her dagger shaking as she caught the edge of the obsidian sword, the impact sending a shockwave of pain through her arm. She stumbled back, gasping for breath, her heart hammering in her chest. The wound he'd inflicted on her side pulsed with burning heat, but she couldn't afford to focus on it—not when Kaelen was standing before her, the shadows wrapped around him like a cloak of malevolent power.

He was no longer the man she had known. The Kaelen she had trusted, the one who had once protected her from the storm, was gone. What stood before her now was something darker, more dangerous. The once clear line between light and shadow had blurred, and it had consumed him.

The Fall of Night

"You're making a mistake, Kaelen," she said through gritted teeth, the words slipping past her pain. "This isn't you. I know you."

He stepped closer, the dark power around him coiling tighter, responding to his every command. The room seemed to bend and twist under its weight. "You never knew me, Lyra," Kaelen's voice was low, a whisper of cold wind against her skin. "You never knew what I was capable of. You think you understand the darkness inside us. You think you can fight it." His eyes narrowed, the flickering light reflecting off the obsidian blade in his hand. "But you've always been weak, Lyra. You've always been afraid of what you are. What you've become."

Her pulse raced. The words cut deeper than the physical pain. Weak. She had fought so hard, struggled to control the light and dark inside her, and yet, now, Kaelen—her companion, her ally—saw only weakness.

"You were never supposed to be my enemy," she said, the words tearing from her lips. "But this—this is your choice, Kaelen. You chose to fall."

He didn't answer. His gaze, once warm and full of purpose, now looked at her with a cold, calculating intensity. There was no hint of recognition in his eyes, no glimmer of the man he used to be. Just the darkness, consuming him, as it had always threatened to do.

The storm outside raged louder, the wind howling through the cracks of the fortress, rattling the walls as if the heavens themselves were in revolt. The air in the room grew thick, heavier, as if the very atmosphere was charged with the energy of the conflict. Lyra's breath came in shallow gasps, her hand still clutching the hilt of her dagger, but she knew she couldn't keep this up forever. The darkness around Kaelen was closing in on her, suffocating her with each passing second.

She needed to act. Now.

Lyra sprang forward, aiming for his exposed side with a speed she hadn't realized she had, but Kaelen was faster, his movements predatory. He parried the blow with ease, knocking her dagger aside, and spun, delivering a swift kick to her stomach that sent her crashing to the cold stone floor. The wind was knocked from her lungs, and for a moment, everything went dark.

She gasped for air, trying to push herself up, but the shadows around Kaelen seemed to swirl, blocking her vision, distorting the world into a fevered, suffocating blur. Her muscles screamed in protest as she struggled to stand, to move, to fight.

"You can't win," Kaelen's voice came from above, cold and cruel. "This is my world now. You never stood a chance."

But his words, though sharp, didn't penetrate the veil of determination that had settled over her heart. She could feel the light—flickering, weak, but it was still there. The light she had chosen. She had always been afraid of it, afraid of what it meant, but now? Now, she understood.

The Fall of Night

The storm outside crackled with thunder, its fury mirroring the battle inside her. She had walked this path before. She had fought this battle in her soul, balancing between light and dark. But the choice had always been hers, and it was hers again.

With a fierce roar, Lyra surged to her feet, her hand gripping the dagger again, the blade steady in her hand. Her breath was labored, but her resolve had never been stronger.

"I will fight you, Kaelen," she said, her voice raw, but firm. "I will never let you destroy everything I've worked for."

Kaelen's eyes flashed with something unreadable. The shadows around him seemed to swell, thickening with each passing second, but Lyra could feel it too—the resistance, the fight inside her that had never truly gone away. She could feel the light pushing back, the defiance rising within her.

"You think you can stop me?" Kaelen's voice was laced with amusement, but there was an edge to it now. He could see the determination in her, but he thought it was useless, just as he had always believed.

Lyra stepped forward, her movements swift, almost graceful despite the weight of the power inside her. She didn't hesitate. This was her moment.

Kaelen raised his sword, ready to strike, but Lyra's eyes locked onto his, a flash of light gleaming in her gaze. The shadows around him surged, but she moved faster, her blade cutting through the air with a sharpness that left a trail of light in its wake. Her dagger collided with the obsidian sword, the force of the blow shaking the ground beneath them, but this time, she held her ground. The power inside her surged with a force she hadn't anticipated, as if the very air around her was pushing back against the darkness.

Kaelen staggered back, surprised by her strength, his eyes narrowing in disbelief. "How?" he whispered, his voice full of hatred and confusion.

Lyra didn't answer. She didn't need to. She had already made her choice. She had already chosen the light, chosen to fight with everything she had, to protect what she loved, to protect herself.

With a fierce cry, she lunged forward again, her movements swift and precise. She saw the hesitation in his eyes, the brief flicker of doubt that crossed his face, but it was too late. With a final thrust, her dagger found its mark—piercing through the darkness that surrounded him, the light shining bright as it struck the heart of the shadows.

For a moment, everything went still. The storm outside ceased, the thunder dying in the distance, and the shadows around Kaelen receded, retreating like a tide pulled back into the sea. His sword fell from his hand with a clang, his body shaking as the power that had once consumed him began to unravel.

Kaelen's eyes locked onto hers, the fear in them palpable, but there was no anger, no defiance. Only the hollow, broken remnants of the man he had once been.

The Fall of Night

Lyra stood over him, her chest rising and falling with each ragged breath. The storm had passed, but the damage had already been done. Kaelen was no longer the man she had known. He was a shadow, a ghost of his former self, and the darkness that had once consumed him was now gone.

But as Lyra looked down at him, she didn't feel triumph. She didn't feel victory. She felt emptiness, a deep, aching void that she knew would never be filled. The battle had ended, but the cost had been far greater than she had ever anticipated.

"Why, Kaelen?" she whispered, her voice breaking. "Why did it have to be this way?"

But Kaelen didn't answer. His eyes were empty, his body limp, and the shadows that had once clung to him were gone.

Lyra turned away, her hand still trembling from the power she had unleashed. The world was quiet now, too quiet, and the weight of everything that had happened—everything she had lost—settled heavily on her shoulders.

The night was still, but Lyra knew that the dawn would never come again. Not for her. Not for Kaelen.

And the light she had fought to preserve? She wasn't sure if it was enough to rebuild the world they had broken.

But she would try. She would always try.

The fall of night was over. But the dawn? It had already passed.

Fifteen

The Last Light

Lyra stood at the edge of the precipice, the ground beneath her feet trembling with the echo of the battle she had just fought. The storm that had raged throughout the night had passed, but the remnants of its fury still lingered in the air. The wind howled through the broken ruins of the Silver King's fortress, rattling the skeletal remains of towers that had once stood tall and proud. Now, they were nothing more than jagged silhouettes against the dawn, a testament to the destruction that had been wrought.

Her breath came in short, shallow gasps as she stared into the vast emptiness before her. The cliff dropped away into the dark chasm below, the depths hidden in shadow. It was as if the world had been split in two, leaving a void where once there had been a future.

The Last Light

And yet, despite the devastation, Lyra could feel something—something deep within her chest—flickering like a dying ember. The light.

She had fought so hard for it, had bled for it, and now, in the aftermath of everything that had transpired, it felt fragile—almost as if it were slipping through her fingers.

Kaelen's face flashed in her mind. His betrayal. His fall. The final confrontation, where she had pierced the darkness within him, ending the war between the light and the shadows that had consumed both their lives. She had thought that would be the end—that the light would shine bright again, that she would be free of the chains that had bound her.

But now, standing here at the edge, the truth settled in like a weight pressing down on her heart. She had won the battle, but the war was far from over.

The light was not the beacon of hope she had believed it to be. It was a fragile thread, stretched thin between light and dark, ready to snap. She had fought for it, yes. But at what cost?

A rustle behind her broke her thoughts, and Lyra whipped around, her dagger instinctively sliding into her hand. Her heart stuttered as her eyes locked onto the figure emerging from the shadows.

It was him.

The figure stepped into the light—tall, draped in a cloak that billowed with the remnants of the storm, his features hidden beneath the hood. But Lyra knew him. She knew that presence. She knew that gaze.

Kaelen.

He was not dead. Not truly.

Her heart skipped a beat. The world seemed to freeze around them, the wind dying down as if the earth itself was holding its breath. Kaelen's eyes—dark, empty—met hers, and in that moment, the world felt impossibly heavy. The darkness around him had not faded. It lingered, a thick shadow that pressed against her like an invisible weight.

"What are you doing here?" she whispered, her voice shaking with disbelief and fear.

Kaelen stood silent for a long moment, his expression unreadable. When he spoke, his voice was distant, almost hollow. "I never left, Lyra. Not really. You should have known that."

Lyra's grip on her dagger tightened, her pulse quickening. "I killed you," she said, the words choking in her throat. "I ended it. I stopped you."

Kaelen's lips curled into something like a smile, but there was no warmth in it. "You ended nothing. You've only delayed the inevitable."

He stepped closer, the shadows around him deepening with

The Last Light

every movement, as though they were an extension of his very being. Lyra took a step back, her mind spinning with confusion and horror. She had seen Kaelen fall. She had felt the light burst through him, had felt the power surge and collapse in on itself, vanquishing the darkness. But now... now he stood before her, a twisted echo of the man he once was.

"You're not Kaelen," she whispered, more to herself than to him. "You can't be."

Kaelen's eyes narrowed, his gaze sharp and filled with a kind of sorrow she hadn't expected. "I was always Kaelen. I was always the one who had to make the hard choices. You just never saw the truth."

Lyra's heart twisted as she heard the words she had feared. The truth.

"You used me," she spat, her voice rising with anger. "You lied to me. You made me think I was helping you, that we were fighting for something real. But it was all a lie. I was nothing but a pawn in your game!"

A flicker of something crossed Kaelen's face—regret? Pain? But it was gone before she could be sure. His hand rose slowly, palm outstretched, as if to reach for her. The shadows around him rippled in response, swirling like an ancient, forgotten force that had never truly gone away.

"You don't understand," Kaelen said quietly, his voice low and almost gentle now. "I never wanted this for you. I never wanted you to have to choose between light and dark. But the world demands it. The balance is broken, Lyra. And you are the key to fixing it. You always have been."

Lyra shook her head, stepping back again. "I won't fix anything. Not like this. Not with you."

The wind howled again, the storm rearing its ugly head once more, as though the heavens themselves were responding to the tension between them. The air grew thick, the shadows around Kaelen crawling, inching closer. They pressed against Lyra like a suffocating blanket, urging her to let go, to give in to the darkness, to forget the fight, to forget the light.

"No," she whispered to herself, her hands trembling. "I won't."

Kaelen's gaze softened, but there was no warmth in it. His eyes—dark and filled with an intensity that she couldn't quite place—remained locked on hers. "You have to, Lyra. This is who you are. This is who we are. There is no turning back now."

Lyra's breath caught in her throat as she realized what he was saying. This wasn't just about him. It wasn't just about the game they had been playing, about the fight for power. No, this was about the very essence of her existence, the balance between light and dark that had defined everything she had ever known.

The storm, the wind, the shadows—they all whispered, urging her to let go. To fall into the abyss.

The Last Light

But something inside her flared—fiercer than ever before, stronger than the darkness. The light.

"No," she said again, her voice trembling with defiance. "I won't fall."

She could feel the power building within her, that fragile, dying ember of light that she had fought for so long. It had been a part of her, but now, it was something more. Something stronger. She had chosen it. And she would fight for it. No matter the cost.

Kaelen's eyes hardened, the shadows around him writhing in response. "Then you'll destroy us all, Lyra," he said softly, almost mournfully. "You'll destroy everything we've fought for."

Lyra stood tall, the light within her flaring brighter than the storm itself, a beacon in the darkness. "I'd rather destroy everything than become what you are."

The shadows screamed, the storm raged louder, and for a moment, it felt as though the world was on the verge of tearing apart. The forces inside her clashed, the light and the dark warring against each other, pushing and pulling, stretching to their breaking point. But Lyra stood firm, her eyes never leaving Kaelen's.

"I won't let you break me," she said, her voice unwavering. "And I won't let you take everything I've fought for."

In that moment, she felt it—she felt the light burst through her like a wave of fire, burning through the shadows, burning through the darkness. The storm outside howled, but the light was brighter than it had ever been. The darkness recoiled, shrieking in agony, as Kaelen stumbled back, his hands rising to shield himself from the onslaught.

But it was too late. The light surged forward, sweeping over him, and for the first time in what felt like an eternity, Kaelen's eyes widened in shock. The shadows around him collapsed, consumed by the light.

The wind died down. The storm ceased.

And in the silence that followed, Lyra stood alone, her heart pounding, the light still flickering in her chest.

She had won. She had chosen the light.

But at what cost?

www.ingramcontent.com/pod-product-compliance
Lightning Source LLC
LaVergne TN
LVHW020424080526
838202LV00055B/5032